1306
Robert kills
John Comyn
of Badenoch
and is crowned
King of Scots

1309
King Robert
holds his first
parliament at
St Andrews

1311
Bruce
begins raids
in the north of
England

1314
Edward Bruce
gets agreement
that Stirling Castle
will surrender by
midsummer if not
relieved by the
English

1320
The
Declaration
of Arbroath
articulates
Scotland's
desire for
freedom

1329
Robert
dies, old
and battle-
scarred
but with
his throne
secure

1310   1320 1330

1306
Bruce
loses the
Battle of
Methven

1307
Bruce
returns from
exile and
wins battles
at Glen Trool
and Loudoun
Hill; Edward I
dies

1310
Edward II
campaigns
in Scotland

1313
Edward II
makes plans
to raise an
invasion
force for the
following
summer

1314
23/24 June
**The Battle of
Bannockburn**
King Robert's
army achieve a
resounding victory
over Edward's army

1328
The Treaty
of Edinburgh
recognises
Scottish
independence
and Bruce's
right to be king

Contents

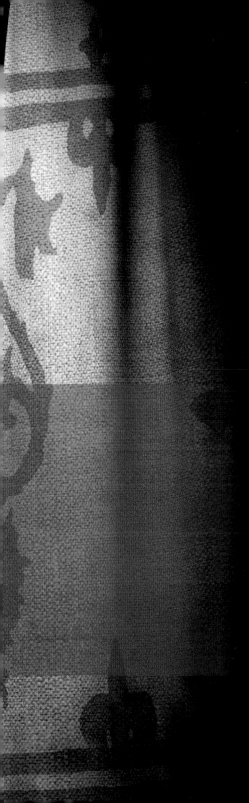

The Battle of BANN⬡CKBURN

Introduction

THE BATTLE OF BANNOCKBURN is the most famous Scots victory – a pivotal moment in Scotland's history, and an icon of Scottish nationhood.

People have visited this site for centuries, to commemorate the thousands of men who fought and died during the battle – a face-down between Robert Bruce, King of Scots, and the English army led by Edward II.

Over the two days of battle, Edward's army was repeatedly thwarted by the Scots' stubborn resistance, before finally finding themselves trapped by the surrounding terrain, with no room to manoeuvre their huge force. The result was an unprecedented rout of King Edward's army. Although it was only one battle in a prolonged conflict, Robert Bruce's remarkable victory has resonated with Scots down the centuries.

The Battle of Bannockburn continues to conjure up ideas of freedom, independence and patriotism; of heroism, perseverance and triumph against overwhelming odds. The modern state-of-the-art interpretation, supported by this souvenir guidebook, will ensure that Bannockburn continues to be commemorated, and that it retains its pride of place in the national consciousness.

'Yet fast they fell, unheard, forgot,
Both Southern fierce and hardy Scot;
And O! amid that waste of life,
What various motives fired the strife!'

Walter Scott, *Lord of the Isles*, 1815

'Qwhen Alexander our kynge was dede ...
Our golde wes changit into lede.'

'When Alexander our king was dead ... Scotland's gold was turned to lead.'

Andrew of Wyntoun, early 15th century

Engraving of Alexander III, c1280, who was King of Scots from 1249–86

Opposite page: the siege of Berwick by Edward I, 1297, from 'St Alban's Chronicle' (15th century); the Stone of Destiny lay under the Coronation Chair at Westminster Abbey before its return to Scotland

Right: a 14th-century French miniature showing John Balliol offering homage to King Edward I

Below: John Balliol, from the Forman Armorial c1562, wearing a tabard bearing the Scottish arms, with a broken sceptre and crown to show his deposition

Who shall be king? 1286–95

The story of Bannockburn starts with a king being thrown from his horse during a storm in his haste to be with his new young second wife.

With Alexander III lying dead at the foot of a cliff near Kinghorn in Fife in 1286, Scotland found itself without the prospect of a king to succeed to the throne. Alexander's nearest heir was his granddaughter Margaret, the 'Maid of Norway'. Soon it was decided that she should marry her cousin Edward, son of the English king, Edward I. Their children would rule both England and Scotland, securing lasting peace between the two countries and ending the threat of civil war in Scotland among competing rivals to the throne. Unfortunately, the young princess died on her way to Scotland in 1290.

The two chief claimants to the vacant throne were Robert Bruce of Annandale – grandfather of the future king, known as the Competitor – and John Balliol, who both claimed descent from David I. The nobles turned to Edward I as an experienced and respected monarch to arbitrate between the claimants. The English king seized his opportunity, arriving with a sizeable force just south of the border at Norham Castle. He insisted that the Scots recognise him as overlord of Scotland and hand over several castles until the kingship was settled. The Scots tried to stall him, but without a clear leader had little option but to comply; Edward had already made the candidates swear homage and fealty to him as a condition of entry to the competition. After nearly 18 months, in November 1292 John Balliol was judged to be the rightful king because he came from the senior line.

However, Balliol proved either unwilling to accept or incapable of standing up to Edward's demands as overlord. So in 1295 a council of 12 Scottish nobles and bishops led by the Comyns, the most important family in Scotland, took control of government. They concluded a treaty with the king of France that each would help the other against England.

Sack, siege and skirmish 1296–1305

Edward rightly suspected that the Scots were colluding with the French and prepared for war. At the head of an army perhaps about 20,000 strong he marched north and sacked Berwick, then Scotland's largest town and an important international trading port, which had shut its gates against him. According to one tradition, he only ordered an end to the slaughter on hearing of a woman murdered while in the act of childbirth. Edward's army went on to destroy a Scottish force at the Battle of Dunbar. The Wars of Independence had begun.

When King John surrendered, the royal insignia was stripped from his tunic in a humiliating public ceremony, supposedly earning him the nickname 'toom tabard' (empty coat). He was then sent to the Tower of London. To make the point that Scotland was no longer an independent kingdom, Edward seized all the documents and regalia of Scotland, including the Stone of Destiny, on which Scots kings had traditionally been inaugurated. It was to remain under the Coronation Chair in Westminster Abbey until 1950, when it was briefly liberated by a group of patriotic Scots, and was formally returned to Scotland in 1996.

With Balliol deposed, the leading Scots nobles dead or in prison and his own men now governing Scotland, Edward did not expect any opposition and prepared to deal with France. The Scots, however, were angered by Edward's demands for men and money to fight his foreign war. Robert Wishart, Bishop of Glasgow, was crucial in co-ordinating the resistance.

Rebellion broke out in several parts of Scotland, with risings in the north under Andrew Murray and in the south-west by William Wallace. While the future king Robert Bruce, Earl of Carrick, and Wishart negotiated terms with the English in 1297, Wallace continued to attack English strongholds. After he and Murray defeated an army led by Edward's lieutenant, the Earl of Surrey, at Stirling Bridge in 1297, Wallace was appointed Guardian of Scotland.

5

Report of trial of William Wallace, 1305

Stained glass window of William Wallace at the National Wallace Monument, Stirling

Constructed in the 1860s on the summit of Abbey Craig, near Stirling, the National Wallace Monument offers impressive views of the surrounding countryside from the top

War with France meant that Edward was on the continent, but he returned home early in 1298. That summer he marched north with an army of over 25,000 men. In a particularly brutal form of defence, Wallace laid waste to southern Scotland in the path of the English in an attempt to prevent them getting supplies and starve them out. But spies alerted Edward to Wallace's position and the English marched quickly to meet the Scots outside Falkirk where a combination of archers and cavalry charges won the day for Edward. Wallace escaped but resigned as Guardian.

Despite Edward's victory, Scotland did not fall to the English king and he spent the next few years trying to extend his grip on southern Scotland. Meanwhile the Scots persuaded the French and the Pope to support their cause, and in 1299 Edward was forced to release King John into papal custody. The Guardians were now John Comyn of Badenoch and Robert Bruce, Earl of Carrick, representing two great and opposing factions in Scotland. By 1301 many expected that King John would soon return to Scotland with an army; this proved too much for Robert Bruce who changed his allegiance to Edward.

However, the following year both the French king and the Pope needed Edward's friendship for different reasons, leaving the Scots without allies. In 1303 Edward took his army north of the Forth for the first time since 1296 and at the end of that year Comyn, now sole Guardian, negotiated for peace on behalf of those still fighting.

The one exception was Wallace, who was outlawed. In 1305 he was captured, tried for treason in London, and hung, drawn and quartered. The war appeared to be over.

Top: portrait of William Wallace by an unknown 19th-century artist

Bottom: late 15th-century manuscript copy of Blind Harry's epic poem The Wallace

Robert fights for his kingdom 1306–13

Like many in Scotland, the Bruce family held land on both sides of the border, but they also made a claim to the Scottish throne after Alexander III's death. Though they supported Edward I in 1296, hoping to be given the kingship once it had been taken from Balliol, they were disappointed. Although his father remained loyal to Edward, Robert Bruce, the Earl of Carrick, became a leader of the 1297 rebellion and briefly joint Guardian of Scotland with rival John 'the Red' Comyn. However, the two men did not get on and frequently quarrelled.

In 1306 Robert and the 'Red' Comyn met on the neutral and sacred ground of Greyfriars Church in Dumfries. What began as an argument between two hot-headed young rivals ended with Comyn stabbed to death in front of the high altar. This sacrilegious crime earned Robert automatic excommunication from the church. Edward ordered his forces 'to burn and slay and raise dragon', and to show no mercy to Bruce's supporters. The Comyns and their allies joined the English to try to exact revenge.

Robert could not have been in a worse position; he knew that there was no going back. The Bishop of Glasgow absolved him for slaying Comyn and hastily arranged for him to be inaugurated as king at Scone on 25 March 1306.

However, Robert's control of the country was far from secure. After being defeated by Aymer de Valence, future Earl of Pembroke, at Methven in June 1306, he fled, possibly to Ireland, to plan his comeback. A Walter Scott-inspired legend has it that the fugitive king took heart from watching a spider trying again and again to cast its web across a seemingly impossible gap. Personal loss must have fuelled Robert's resolve; he lost friends, allies and family during these early years, including three of his brothers who were brutally executed.

Suffering for the cause

Women also played a part in the Wars of Independence. Isabel, Countess of Buchan, crowned Robert at Scone, as her family held the hereditary right to perform the ceremony. She and Robert's wife, daughter and sisters were captured in September 1306. Most were imprisoned in England but Countess Isabel and Robert's sister Mary suffered a harsher ordeal. They were confined for four years in wooden cages on the towers of Berwick and Roxburgh castles as an example to others.

Left: the Countess of Buchan crowns Bruce, by Morris Meredith Williams (1881–1973)

Robert returned from exile in 1307, raising supporters from his family heartlands in Carrick and Annan and from the Western Isles to conduct a successful guerrilla campaign, as well as defeating an English force in a skirmish at Glen Trool. In May 1307, just before he won the Battle of Loudoun Hill, he was joined by young James Douglas, who was angry because Edward refused to return the lands which he had stripped from his father for rebelling against him. Although at first he wavered, James reckoned he had more to gain by supporting Bruce. He proved to be a master of the daring raid and ambush, a fearless fighter at Bannockburn and a lifelong friend.

By now old and ill, Edward I made one last attempt to crush Bruce and re-establish his rule. It was too late. He died just before reaching the Solway Firth, which marked the border between the two countries. His son, Edward II, was a very different character. He had inherited enormous debts from his father, but angered his barons by lavishing gifts and an earldom on his favourite, Piers Gaveston. Edward's difficulties with his rebellious nobles gave Robert respite to overcome the Comyns and other Balliol supporters. By 1309 he was strong enough to hold his first parliament at St Andrews, and a year later the 'Declaration of the Clergy' was issued in support of Bruce's campaign against the English and to justify his kingship.

Edward mounted an invasion in 1310 to avoid dealing with his political problems at home. However, he was unable to find Robert and, though he gave heart to his supporters in Scotland, achieved little. Now Robert's men began to make increasingly bold raids across the border. Edward's Scottish strongholds also began to fall – Perth, Dundee, Roxburgh, Linlithgow and Edinburgh. By 1314 only Berwick and Stirling held out.

Declaration by the bishops, abbots, priors and other Scottish clergy asserting the right of King Robert I to the Scottish Crown and swearing fealty and allegiance to him, 24 February 1310

Contemporary illustration of Edward II sitting on a throne, with a second figure offering him a crown, probably the crown of Scotland

Secret warfare

'Hush ye, hush ye, little pet ye,
Hush ye, hush ye, do not fret ye,
The Black Douglas shall not get ye.'

Traditional lullaby sung by mothers in north-east England

In the years before Bannockburn Robert waged a guerrilla war, known at the time as 'secret warfare'. He employed blackmail to build his war chest. One of Edward's Scottish supporters complained that he had paid the enormous sum of £2,000 to prevent Robert from laying waste his land.

The Scots were determined to secure freedom, whatever the cost or personal sacrifice. Robert's men adopted hit and run tactics, taking castles by surprise in daring night raids. Captured castles were destroyed to save the expense of garrisoning them as well as denying them to the English. In a ruthless scorched earth policy, his troops burned crops and slaughtered livestock to ensure they would never feed the opposition.

The episode known as the Douglas Larder shows the single-mindedness and barbarity of Bruce's men. In 1307 James Douglas and a band of supporters attacked his own family seat, Douglas Castle in Lanarkshire. When most of the garrison were at Mass on Palm Sunday, Douglas struck, capturing those in the castle and the rest when they returned. He then massacred them, piling their heads on top of the food stores which he set on fire. He salted the wells, down which he had thrown the rotting corpses of horses, and torched the castle, causing considerable damage.

In fact, this story is unlikely to be true and Douglas did not actually recapture his castle until later, around 1309, but the point is that many people believed he was capable of it.

Right: Douglas Castle in South Lanarkshire was once a stronghold of the Douglas family. The earliest castle was built in the 13th century and was destroyed and rebuilt several times over the centuries; this ruined tower is all that remains of the 17th-century castle

From siege to showdown 1313–14

Capturing Stirling Castle was the key to controlling Scotland. Perched on its defensive crag, it guarded the crossing of the River Forth and the main route north. Stirling, 'the brooch of Scotland', was the strategic centre of the country.

By 1314 the castle had already changed sides five times and by May was under siege by Robert's brother, Edward. Its Scottish governor, Sir Philip Mowbray, negotiated a deal with Edward Bruce that he would hand over the castle if he was not relieved by an English army by midsummer's day. However, King Edward had been planning to march north for many months, and King Robert was busy training his men nearby, so this agreement made sure that Stirling would be the focus of the upcoming campaign.

This time, too, Robert had a reason to fight. In October 1313, he had felt in sufficient control of Scotland to issue the threat that anyone who did not accept him as king within a year would forfeit their lands. If he did not do battle with Edward's army, this would give heart to those Scots who held out against him and he would be unable to enforce this ultimatum.

The English army mustered at Wark near Berwick before crossing the River Tweed into Scotland. King Edward had called on his lords to fulfil their feudal obligation to provide a specific number of troops and wrote to county sheriffs to choose a quota of foot soldiers for the muster. Although loyal men such as the Earl of Gloucester brought their substantial retinues with them, four earls disobeyed Edward's summons and stayed away. They sent the minimum number of men that they were obliged to provide under the terms of their oath of loyalty to the king, or promised cash instead of service. A fleet was commandeered to sail north with additional provisions.

'He who holds Stirling, holds Scotland.'

Traditional saying

Blàr Allt a' Bhonnaich, the Battle of the Burn of Bannock

In the 14th century, Scotland was a multi-ethnic society, its population made up of people whose ancestors were English, Irish, Flemish, French, Welsh and Scandinavian. While Scots was commonly spoken, half of its inhabitants spoke Gaelic, including those in Robert's earldom of Carrick in south-west Scotland.

Edward's men, who included Gascons (he was Duke of Gascony, a region in south-west France) and a few Germans, between them spoke at least four languages. On both sides of the border regional accents and dialects were also much more distinctive than today.

The troops made a long, weary journey by land and sea from all parts of England, Wales, Ireland and further afield. Some soldiers deserted en route, hiding in woods until the army passed. At Wark the men saw for themselves the devastation which Robert's raids had inflicted. For many, the first sight of Scotland would have confirmed rumours of the ruthless resolve of the Scots.

In total it is estimated that the arrivals were 7,000 short of the original call-up. Despite this, when finally assembled it was the largest army to march into Scotland since the time of Edward I.

It was the ninth time that an army had crossed the border since 1296. With midsummer only a week away, Edward's army finally left Wark and Berwick and faced a gruelling march to reach Stirling Castle by the deadline. The men won a two-day respite in Edinburgh as fresh supplies were unloaded from the ships in Leith and stragglers and late arrivals caught up. Then they were off again early on 22 June to cover the 20 difficult miles to Falkirk. By the afternoon of the 23rd the exhausted foot soldiers arrived 9 miles short of their goal, their throats parched and their shoes in tatters.

Meanwhile, Robert had been training his men in Torwood Forest, which lay between Falkirk and Stirling. He had assembled his men in May, with days at the training camp spent drilling and nights in the open air. But as the English army approached, Robert moved his men into the New Park, the royal forest to the south of Stirling Castle, near to the road on which Edward was travelling.

The baggage train

Edward's baggage train was said to contain so many wagons that had they been placed end to end the column would have stretched for 20 miles. The king's Italian merchant, Antonio Pessagno, had masterminded the collection of huge quantities of supplies at Berwick. Much had been brought there by sea. There was wheat and flour for bread, oats for the horses and barley for brewing. The men expected not only food, but also a gallon of ale or wine a day.

Edward was encumbered with all the paraphernalia of an occupying army as well as a travelling court. Top knights brought their retinue of servants and nobles had packed extensively, even for the short time they expected to spend in southern Scotland.

The Great Seal of Edward II, the principal seal of royal authority. Great seals depicted the monarch on their throne on one side, and on horseback on the reverse

'for the capture of his castles Edward could scarcely restrain his tears. He summoned the earls and barons to come to his aid and overcome the traitor who called himself King.'

Vita Edwardi Secundi, 1326

Robert I

Born: 1274

Background: Of noble birth on both sides of his family, little is known of his childhood. Aged 18, he received the earldom of Carrick from his father. The Bruces sided with Edward I against Balliol, whom they considered had less right to the throne than them.

Most likely spoke: Gaelic, Scots, English and Norman French.

Married: Isabel, the 16-year-old daughter of the Earl of Mar. She died in 1296 shortly after the birth of a daughter, Marjorie Bruce, from whom the Stewart dynasty was to trace its lineage. Robert's second wife was Elizabeth, daughter of the 2nd Earl of Ulster, with whom he had four children.

Became king: 1306

Challenges: Robert had to win the loyalty of his people and bring them together in a united cause, namely a comprehensive victory over the English.

Verdict: He went down in history as 'Good King Robert'. Near contemporaries praised not only his strength and fearlessness but also his humanity and courage.

He was undoubtedly ambitious and sometimes ruthless in gaining his ends and many Scots at the time hated him. Today, military historians admire his mastery of tactics and use of the landscape, and Scots celebrate him as one of their greatest heroes.

Edward II

Born: 1284

Background: Sixth in the Plantagenet line of English kings. His father gave him the title of Prince of Wales in 1301.

Spoke: Norman French and English.

Married: Isabella, the only surviving daughter of Philip IV of France, in 1308. She was known for her beauty, intelligence and diplomatic skills.

Became king: 1307

Challenges: Edward I was a hard act to follow. Edward felt duty-bound to carry on his father's unfinished business in Scotland. He also inherited an empty war chest.

Edward was virtually at war with his own barons. This vulnerable and insecure young man surrounded himself with favourites, notably Piers Gaveston, and he was grief-stricken when his barons had Gaveston murdered. An uneasy truce was established in 1312.

Despite being trained in military crafts from childhood, Edward preferred boating, swimming and 'rustic pursuits', such as digging ditches or thatching roofs, to soldiering.

Verdict: History has not been kind to Edward, who was the first English king to be deposed since the Norman Conquest.

Heraldry

Coats of arms signalled loyalties like football scarves today. Knights displayed their lord's colours on their shield, as a shoulder badge, on their surcoat over their armour, and on their horse's caparison. In the heat of battle, colours flagged up who was where and advertised to the enemy that a knight was worth taking alive for his ransom.

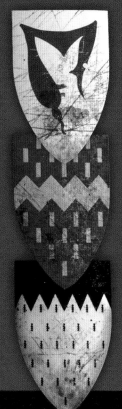

Preparing for battle 1314

The make-up of the armies

No-one knows exactly how large the two armies were. Robert had around 6,000 men, while it is estimated that Edward's troops numbered around 18,000. Edward had more than 2,000 knights to Robert's 500 horsemen and his infantry probably outnumbered Robert's by nearly three to one. As well as fighting men, there were the camp followers who kept the army on the road – clerks, paymasters, cooks, blacksmiths, seamstresses, ale wives and prostitutes – whose numbers may have equalled or even exceeded that of the troops.

Whatever the headcount, it was truly a David and Goliath affair.

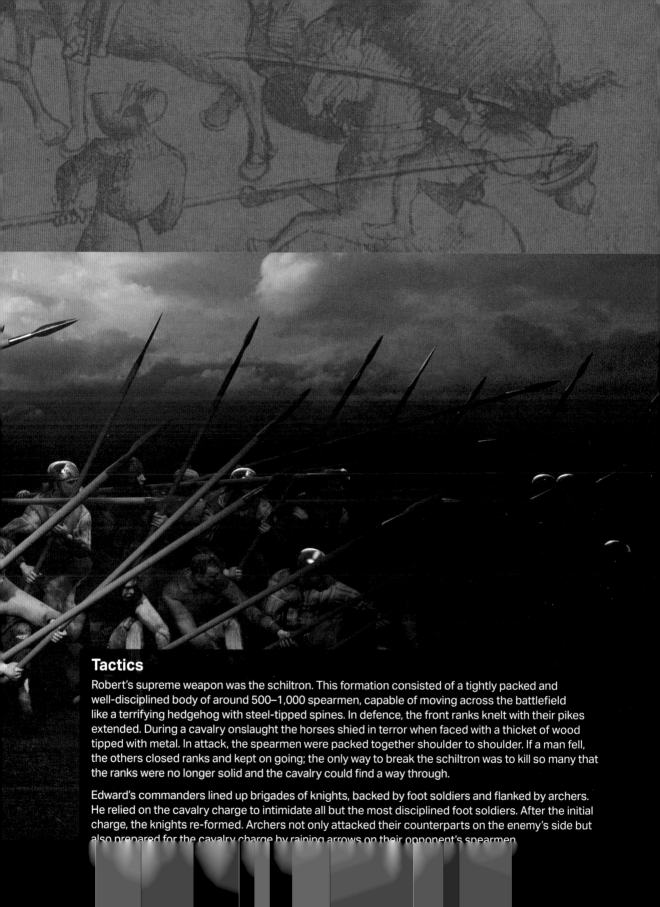

Tactics

Robert's supreme weapon was the schiltron. This formation consisted of a tightly packed and well-disciplined body of around 500–1,000 spearmen, capable of moving across the battlefield like a terrifying hedgehog with steel-tipped spines. In defence, the front ranks knelt with their pikes extended. During a cavalry onslaught the horses shied in terror when faced with a thicket of wood tipped with metal. In attack, the spearmen were packed together shoulder to shoulder. If a man fell, the others closed ranks and kept on going; the only way to break the schiltron was to kill so many that the ranks were no longer solid and the cavalry could find a way through.

Edward's commanders lined up brigades of knights, backed by foot soldiers and flanked by archers. He relied on the cavalry charge to intimidate all but the most disciplined foot soldiers. After the initial charge, the knights re-formed. Archers not only attacked their counterparts on the enemy's side but also prepared for the cavalry charge by raining arrows on their opponent's spearmen.

Knights

Sons of the nobility, knights were trained from childhood to ride, fight and use a sword. They were usually sent from home to serve as a personal servant to a lord before becoming a squire, then a knight. Some were knighted on the field of battle, but most went through an elaborate ceremony. After a night of prayer and confession, his lord would tap him on the shoulder with a sword, as a sign that he accepted the obligations of knighthood. He was expected to be loyal, courteous, brave and pious, although the reality was often very different. In 1306 Edward I created 300 knights during the Feast of the Swans. Their number included his son and the son of John Comyn, who never forgave Robert Bruce for killing his father. These knights swore revenge on Robert.

Foot soldiers

There was a much higher ratio of foot soldiers to knights, particularly in Robert's army. His men had the advantage of training and discipline as all ranks, from nobles to tenant farmers, fought together on foot. Many were hardened veterans of years of guerrilla fighting.

The higher ranks of Edward's army fought alongside each other in the cavalry, while the foot soldiers were organised into groups of 20, which then came together to form a cohort of 100, each with their own leaders.

Archers

Robert had far fewer archers than Edward, who sourced thousands of longbowmen from Wales, Ireland and the Midlands. His Welsh contingent not only provided archers, but also knife-men trained to hunt and stab prey on difficult terrain.

War horses

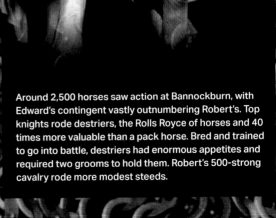

Around 2,500 horses saw action at Bannockburn, with Edward's contingent vastly outnumbering Robert's. Top knights rode destriers, the Rolls Royce of horses and 40 times more valuable than a pack horse. Bred and trained to go into battle, destriers had enormous appetites and required two grooms to hold them. Robert's 500-strong cavalry rode more modest steeds.

The lie of the land

What lay under the soldiers' feet was critical to the outcome of the battle. The landscape of rivers, moorland, forest, scrub, farmland and marsh was very different from today.

The Roman road was built around AD80 or later to carry marching legions from their camps around Falkirk to the crossing of the Forth at Stirling and onwards north. It was still traceable in the early 14th century.

Torwood Forest, where Robert set up his training camp, stretched nearly all the way from Falkirk to the boggy land around the Bannock Burn. Its crags had a good view of the Roman road through the forest.

The New Park was reserved for hunting. Blocking the entry to the New Park, the core of Robert's army lined up just inside the woodland between the Bannock Burn and the Borestone, a rock with a hole in it which is thought to be where Bruce raised his standard. The area near St Ninian's Kirk and the

Borestone provided vantage points over the low ground of the Carse, while those camp followers, or sma' folk, who were not part of the army gathered nearby, which tradition today says was behind Gillies Hill.

Part of the Carse, where Edward camped overnight and where much of the action of the second day of the battle may have taken place, was a peatbog beside the meanders of the River Forth. Intersected by ditches and tidal streams, the rough terrain would have proved a tough obstacle for the English mounted knights. One source referred to Bannockburn as the 'battle of the pows' [pools].

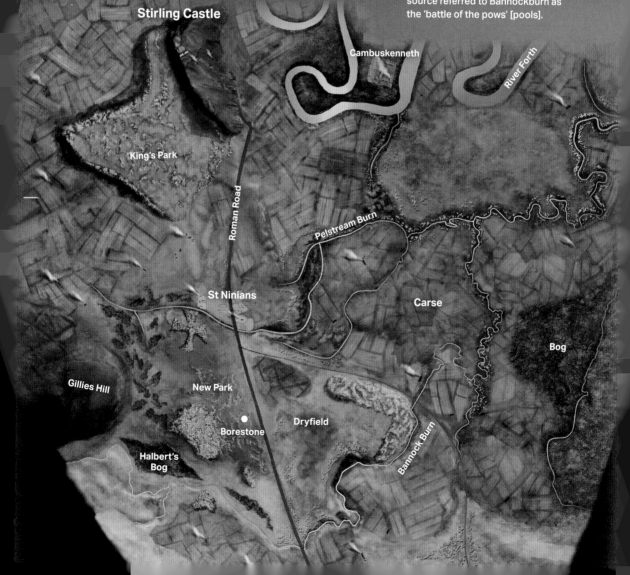

Stirling Castle

Cambuskenneth

River Forth

King's Park

Roman Road

Pelstream Burn

St Ninians

Carse

Bog

Gillies Hill

New Park

Borestone

Dryfield

Bannock Burn

Halbert's Bog

The final line-up

Robert divided his army into three divisions commanded by himself, his brother Edward and his nephew Thomas Randolph, the Earl of Moray. James Douglas and Walter Stewart probably fought with Edward Bruce, while Sir Robert Keith was put in charge of the cavalry.

Three earls served under Edward: Humphrey de Bohun, Earl of Hereford; Gilbert de Clare, Earl of Gloucester; and Aymer de Valence, Earl of Pembroke. The army was divided into a number of divisions led by the vanguard. But there were growing signs of tension. The Earl of Gloucester claimed the right to lead the vanguard, as he said his ancestors had done. However, the Earl of Hereford objected, saying that it was his duty as hereditary Constable of England. Edward put them in joint command, which failed to resolve the quarrel.

Let battle commence – 23 June 1314

On 23 and 24 June 1314, against overwhelming odds, Robert routed Edward's army.

Robert made careful preparations. On 22 June, he moved his men to the New Park, 2 miles south of Stirling Castle. He chose his ground wisely. The trees of the hunting reserve beside the road to the castle would make it difficult for Edward to deploy his cavalry, while Halbert's Bog and the rolling hills to the south-west would protect them from attack on that side. Robert wanted to defend his flanks and force Edward's troops to fight his army head on. He prepared the open ground with knee-deep pits, planted with stakes, to trap the horses. Disguised with grass and sticks, ditches also proved a hazard to enemy cavalry.

In the New Park, the day of the 23rd dawned with Mass and a breakfast of bread and water as it was the eve of the saint's day of St John the Baptist. For Edward's troops, it was a quick march from Falkirk towards Stirling. In the early afternoon Sir Philip Mowbray slipped out of Stirling Castle to warn Edward that Robert had blocked the road through the Park and anyway, technically the castle had been relieved. But Edward had no intention of leaving it there.

Many of the young soldiers in the English army were desperate to get to grips with the Scots, who normally avoided pitched battles. Although Edward commanded his army to halt for a break, the vanguard pressed on, either mistaking or ignoring his orders. Robert's spearmen stood firm and the vanguard was repulsed. The Earl of Gloucester was thrown from his horse, although he escaped unharmed.

Early in the engagement, the young knight Henry de Bohun, the Earl of Hereford's nephew, spotted Robert, mounted on a palfrey and armed only with a battle axe, reviewing his forward troops. The gold crown on his helmet gave him away. De Bohun spurred his horse and charged. Robert coolly swerved at the last moment, stood in his stirrups and struck a deadly blow on de Bohun's head, breaking his battle axe in the action. It was a major morale-booster to Robert's troops. However, the incident calls into question Bruce's judgement in placing himself in such a vulnerable position – a different result would have proved disastrous.

'And quhen it cummys to the fycht
Ilk men set hart will and mycht
To stynt our fayis mekill prid.'

'And when it comes to the fight
Let each man set his heart will and strength
To humble our foes' great pride.'

John Barbour, *The Brus*, c1375

Illustration of the 14th-century stained glass window at Tewkesbury Abbey showing Gilbert de Clare, Earl of Gloucester, who was killed at Bannockburn

Two experienced knights, Sir Robert Clifford and Sir Henry de Beaumont, determined to try a flanking movement, taking over 300 horsemen around to the north along the edge of the higher ground, perhaps to get behind Bruce's army and prevent a retreat. Spotting them, Moray – positioned at St Ninian's Kirk to the west – ordered his men into a schiltron, which pushed back the cavalry. At least one English knight was captured. As the cavalry retreated, the first day of battle was effectively over.

After an exhausting day, Edward met with his leaders to discuss what to do next. His commanders were in favour of resting where they were, a direct attack on Robert's well-defended position being seen as suicidal. When the Earl of Gloucester suggested giving the troops time to rest and rethink their plans, Edward accused him of treason. Gloucester prophetically swore that he would fight to the death.

Desperate for water for his men and horses, and wishing to be out of the way of a possible Scottish night attack, Edward decided to cross the Bannock Burn and set up camp for the night on the Carse beyond.

Waiting for dawn – 23/24 June 1314

It took a long time to direct Edward's army across the Bannock Burn. Bridges had to be improvised from whatever timber came to hand – including doors and roofs from local houses – to lead horses across the wider ditches. Supply carts could not negotiate the terrain. Edward's troops spent an uncomfortable night camped on the Carse; some spent the night carousing or panicking about what the day might bring, while others had to wait until nearly daybreak to cross the burn.

Camped in the New Park, Robert had still not made up his mind as to what to do next. Although he had trained his troops for months, he was much more comfortable with hit and run tactics than a pitched battle. On the other hand, Edward's troops had come off worst in no fewer than three encounters earlier that day, which cannot have done much for their confidence. A decisive victory would give Robert control of almost the whole country and of those landowners still loyal to Edward; losing would put in jeopardy his recent gains, including Edinburgh, as well as having to deal with Edward re-occupying southern Scotland.

Robert's resolve was strengthened when Alexander Seton, a landowner in south-east Scotland which, until recently, had been under Edward's command, came over to the Scottish king's side. Seton talked of the low morale and confusion within Edward's camp and put his own neck on the line by promising Robert victory. After consulting his leaders, at dawn Robert ordered an advance as close as possible to Edward's line.

Loyal but to whom?

Alexander Seton was not the only person to switch sides. In 1314 people in general, but nobles in particular, were more motivated by family allegiances, oaths of loyalty and personal gain than by any concept of nationhood. Some families held land on both sides of the border.

Robert himself had changed sides more than once, finally seizing the throne that he viewed as his birthright. In that long night between the two days of battle, the Earl of Atholl, Constable of Scotland, defected to Edward. Did he think that Robert would be defeated or did he bear a grudge against Edward Bruce, who had dishonoured his sister by fathering her child and then deserting her? The earl attacked Robert's supply base at Cambuskenneth Abbey, killed a knight and 'many men', and stole food. After the battle he fled to England.

Above: One of Scotland's greatest treasures, the Monymusk reliquary dates from around AD750 and may have been the Breccbennach carried by Abbot Bernard at Bannockburn. The quigrich (crozier) of St Fillans (right) is thought to date from the 14th century and may also have been carried at the battle

'Let us do or die' – 24 June 1314

Again, the day started with prayers. In this deeply religious time, men saw battle as the judgement of God and sought to make peace and confess their sins in case they did not survive the day. Robert made a speech invoking the support of the saints, knighted James Douglas, among others, and formed his spearmen into three schiltrons. He raised his standard, possibly at the Borestone. Abbot Bernard, the *deoradh*, or keeper of relics, carried a tiny casket – the Breccbennach – which contained a bone of St Columba, to bless the troops. Abbot Maurice of Inchaffray walked at the head of the army, saying mass and blessing the men as they knelt in prayer.

The first to engage were the two sets of archers and it was the Scots who pulled back first. By this time the English cavalry were lined up, though they could not spread out fully into their various divisions because they were constrained by the terrain.

This is the earliest known depiction of the Battle of Bannockburn, from Walter Bower's Scotichronicon, a history of the Scottish nation written in Latin in the 1440s

Remembering how he had been accused of cowardice the previous day, Gloucester charged headlong into the Scots ranks, massed in Edward Bruce's schiltron. Few, if any, followed the earl, who was slain. He would have been worth a huge ransom, but Bruce had ordered that no booty or prisoners were to be taken till battle was won. The English cavalry could not deal with the Scottish infantry, for their charges broke on the spears of the schiltrons. The Earl of Moray and his men advanced in schiltron formation. Horses panicked, and their fallen riders were finished off by axe or sword. With only a limited front, the English were unable to bring their superior numbers to bear, the ranks in the rear being pushed back by their retreating companions. As the battle proceeded, when the schiltrons advanced they proved invincible in their tight formations. But the battle was not yet won.

'The great horses of the English charged the pikes of the Scots, as it were into a dense forest. There arose a great and terrible crash of spears broken and of destriers wounded to the death.'

The Lanercost Chronicle, 14th century

As spearmen attacked Edward's beleaguered cavalry, Aonghas Óg of Islay let loose his men from the Isles. When Aonghas arrived on the battlefield, it is said that Robert greeted him with the words '*is cunbhalach mo dhòchas annad*' (my hope is constant in thee), which became the motto of Clanranald.

Under Sir Robert Keith, the 500-strong Scottish cavalry successfully routed a force of English archers. His attack deprived Edward of what should have been one of his deadliest weapons.

The battle was hard-fought as the two sides engaged in fierce hand-to-hand combat. The English were packed tight together and were unable to take advantage of their greater numbers. Many fell victim to the axes and knives of the Scots, who relished fighting at close quarters; others were driven back to drown in the Bannock Burn.

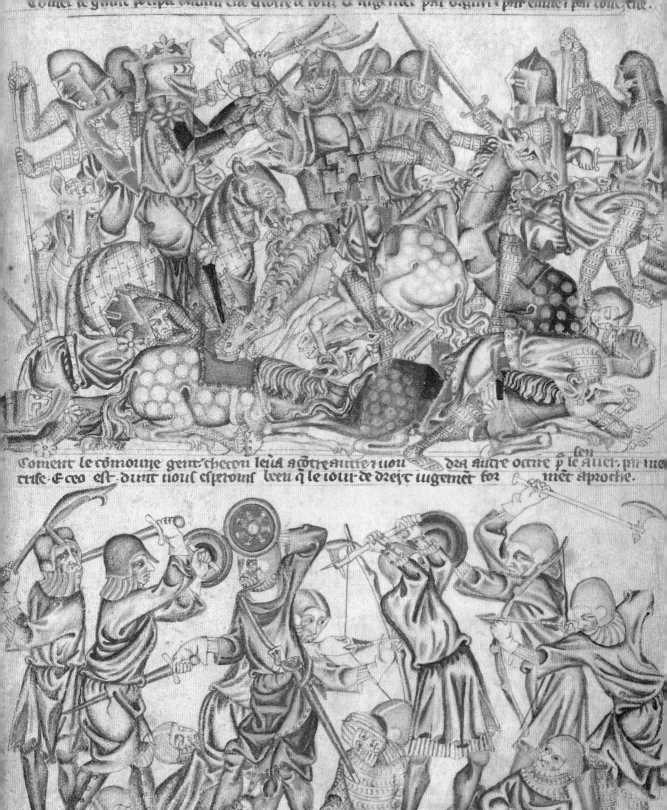

Coment le comoune gent checon leſa aentreamtre vou   ſen
triſe E coo eſt dirnt nouſ eſperonſ beu q le iour de dreit iugemēt for   mēt aproche

A 19th-century engraving depicting Edward II being repulsed from Stirling Castle after the battle

As it became clear that the English were losing the battle, the Earl of Pembroke began to lead Edward away. Sir Giles d'Argentan so feared the shame of retreating that, rather than continue to guard the king, he turned his horse and charged to his death. Edward escaped towards Stirling. Honour-bound to surrender and perhaps fearing that the king would be taken prisoner, Sir Philip Mowbray refused to open the gate. At the head of 60 horsemen, Sir James Douglas allegedly chased Edward south.

Seeing Edward's royal standard leave the field was the trigger for the 'small folk'. These were probably lightly armed irregulars who followed Robert to battle – tenant farmers, townsmen, labourers and latecomers to the Torwood training camp. Local people were less likely to be among the crowd; war meant disruption to their daily lives and some had grown prosperous servicing Edward's garrison in Stirling Castle. According to the 14th-century chronicler John Barbour, the 'small folk' streamed on to the battlefield. Thinking that they were Scottish reinforcements, Edward's men panicked and broke ranks, though some knights fought to the bitter end. The Bannock Burn was filled with the bodies of those trying to flee.

Up close and personal

It is difficult today even to imagine the sights, sounds and smells of medieval battle – the knights charging and the indestructible schiltrons; the clash of sword against shield, the snapping of spears and the cracking of bone against destrier's hoof; the stench of sweat and excrement. All around was the babel of different languages, the barking of orders, the whoop of battle cries – 'Lay on! Lay on! They fail!', 'Slay, slay' – and the agony of dying men.

Opposite: 'Peers and commoners fighting' from the Holkham Bible, c1320-30 – the image of a king wielding a battle axe in the top half has led some historians to link this image to Bannockburn. It illustrates how soldiers would have been equipped in an early 14th-century battle

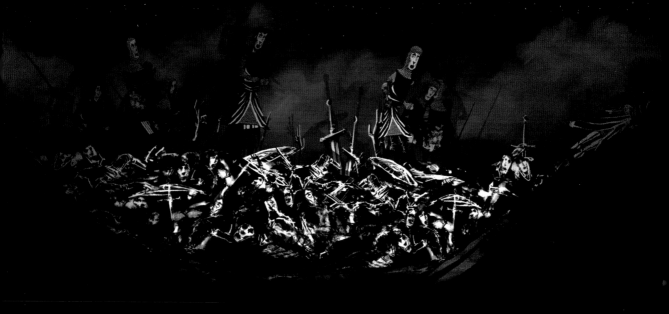

Aftermath 1314

How many died at Bannockburn will never be known, although losses were undoubtedly huge. Ironically, Robert's army probably killed more Scots – in the opposing army – than Edward's did. The numbers of dead and injured had an impact on the conduct of the ensuing war, reducing the ability of the north of England to withstand Scottish raids.

In the hours that followed the battle, Robert's men picked over the heaps of corpses. Plunder was top of their minds as a reward for fighting unpaid for their king. The wine from Edward's baggage train flowed freely as men looted gold, weapons and fine cloth. Many of Edward's troops managed to escape because the Scots were either busily ransacking the baggage train or were too tired to pursue them.

The aftermath of the battle was chaotic. Edward fled without stopping to Dunbar, where he boarded a boat and made for Berwick. It was an ignominious parting from a land which he had been so confident of conquering. Some of Edward's supporters, including the Earl of Hereford and the Anglo-Scottish Earl of Angus, made for Bothwell Castle on the River Clyde, at the time under Edward's control. On hearing of King Robert's victory, the Scots-born keeper of the castle decided to switch to the winning side. After appearing to welcome the earls into the castle, he imprisoned them until they could be handed over for ransom and killed their followers.

> 'an evil, miserable and calamitous day for the English'
>
> *The Lanercost Chronicle, 14th century*

Knights were of more value alive than dead. The Scots took them for ransom money and to trade for prisoners. Robert negotiated the freedom of his wife Elizabeth, daughter Marjorie, and sisters Mary and Christina, and he showed mercy to some knights. Sir Marmaduke Tweng was entertained at dinner after personally surrendering to Robert, having first hidden his armour in a bush. Robert allowed this distant relative by marriage to return in peace to his Yorkshire estate.

A battle in a war 1314-29

Although Bannockburn certainly did not secure peace, its outcome was significant. Apart from the great psychological benefit and prestige it brought for Robert, it also meant that he could enforce his promise that any noble who did not accept him as king would lose their lands, and most now did swear homage. Loot and ransom money helped finance the war effort, while the return of his wife and daughter gave King Robert the possibility of an heir.

The Scots harried further and further into England, some areas having to pay blackmail every year to buy them off. Robert, however, still faced trouble at home. The opposition focused on John Balliol's son, Edward – now living in England – as the rightful king, but a plot to overthrow Robert in 1320 was quickly taken care of.

Although Edward II lost not only his shield and privy seal but also much of his credibility at Bannockburn, he refused to recognise Robert as king until his dying day. Nonetheless Robert reigned in effect over an independent Scotland. In 1318 Berwick, the last English stronghold in Scotland, fell to James Douglas. Its taking angered the Pope, who wanted England and Scotland to stop fighting and go on Crusade, and who now threatened Scotland with excommunication. In 1320 Bruce's nobles were encouraged to seal a letter asking the Pope to lift this excommunication, with a stirring explanation of why they needed to fight behind King Robert for their independence. As the Declaration of Arbroath, this letter has become the most celebrated document in Scottish history.

In the difficult aftermath of the deposition and murder of Edward II, the regency government for Edward III finally recognised Robert as Robert I, King of Scots. A treaty was sealed by Robert in Edinburgh on 17 March 1328, which was ratified by the English parliament sitting in Northampton on 1 May. In return for a much needed £20,000, Edward agreed to treat Scotland as an independent nation ruled by Robert and his heirs. The border between the two countries was restored to the line operating during the reign of Alexander III.

Robert died in Cardross on the Clyde estuary in 1329. At 54, he was now a battle-scarred old man. His son David was only five when he inherited the throne. After Bruce's death the English invaded in an attempt to place John Balliol's son on the throne of Scotland, and David II spent 12 years in prison in England after several defeats. However, the prospect of taking the throne of France, a claim to which he held through his mother, persuaded Edward III to abandon his attempts to conquer Scotland. Although full-scale invasions and cross-border raiding became part and parcel of Anglo-Scottish relations until 1587, the threat of conquest finally receded.

'As long as one hundred of us remain alive, never will we under any conditions be brought under English rule. It is not for glory, nor for riches, nor honours that we are fighting, but for freedom itself, which no honest person gives up but with life itself.'

The Declaration of Arbroath, 1320

Red sulphur cast of the 1st Great Seal of Robert I, showing the king on horseback, c1306

What did Bruce look like?

The ways in which artists have imagined what Robert Bruce looked like reflects their time, the techniques available to them and their creativity.

When the tomb in Dunfermline Abbey thought to be Robert's was opened in 1818, artist William Scouler made a cast of the skull found inside (see below). Pilkington Jackson used this cast as the basis for the face of his statue at Bannockburn.

Robert Bruce as represented on the £20 Clydesdale banknote, 'Famous Scots' series

Late 18th-century engraving

Marble bust in the Hall of Heroes at the National Wallace Monument

Facial reconstruction of the older Bruce created in the late 1990s

From the Forman Armorial, c1562, in a tabard bearing the arms of Scotland and wielding a sword and sceptre

What happened to …

Edward II invaded Scotland for the last time in 1322. His promotion of favourites and troubles with his barons continued until he was deposed in favour of his son, Edward III: he was forced to abdicate and, although there were stories that he escaped, was probably murdered in 1327.

James Douglas became known as 'Good Sir James' or 'the Black Douglas'. He was the heart and soul of the terrifying raids the Scots made across the border. On his deathbed, Robert asked James to take his heart on Crusade. In 1330 Douglas died en route, fighting the Moors at Teba in southern Spain. His companions returned with the casket containing Bruce's heart, which was buried in Melrose Abbey, while James's body was laid to rest at Douglas, Lanarkshire.

Aonghas Óg received the lordship of Lochaber from Robert as a reward for his support. He died in 1330 and was interred on Iona, where the Benedictine monastery had been founded around 1200 by one of his ancestors.

With his brother's support and the backing of the Irish kings, in 1315 Edward Bruce invaded Ireland, then under English rule. He proclaimed himself High King of Ireland, but was killed in battle three years later, along with many of his followers.

Isabel, Countess of Buchan was released from prison in 1310, allowed to stay in a nunnery and just before Bannockburn was handed into the care of her niece, Alicia. Her fate thereafter is unknown.

In 1315 Thomas Randolph, Earl of Moray, accompanied Edward Bruce in invading Ireland. After Robert's death he acted as Regent for the young David II. He fell ill and died in 1332 as he led an army to repel an English invasion under Edward Balliol.

The Earl of Gloucester died in the heat of the battle. His body was taken to a nearby church where King Robert, his brother-in law, spent the night in vigil. Robert then allowed the earl's body to be taken for burial beside his father at Tewkesbury Abbey.

Escaping into the trap at Bothwell Castle, the Earl of Hereford was traded for the release of Robert's wife, sisters and other prominent Scottish prisoners. Despite Edward II paying the ransom, he later lost Hereford's support. Hereford joined the opposition in 1322 and was killed fighting against his king.

The Earl of Pembroke helped lead Edward from the field at Bannockburn. He unsuccessfully tried to keep the peace between Edward and his rebellious barons after Edward adopted a new favourite, Hugh Despenser. He died in 1324 while on a diplomatic mission to France.

Tomb of Edward II at Gloucester Cathedral

Detail of Aonghas Óg's grave slab, which can be seen at Iona Abbey

Effigy of James Douglas on his tomb at St Bride's Church, Douglas

Where was Bannockburn?

Controversy has raged for centuries over where the battlefield actually was. Sometimes the 'where' has taken precedence over the 'why' and the 'what it meant'. Historians have scoured documents for clues, while archaeologists have applied their increasing armoury of tools.

Such a major battle has left tantalisingly few traces. The National Trust for Scotland found a possible arrowhead near the visitor centre in 2004, which probably dates from the 14th century. None of Bruce's pits have been identified and 'wooden stakes from the pits', recovered from Milton Bog in the 19th century, turned out to be the roots of Mesolithic pine trees. No human remains or items of personal equipment, much less mass graves, have been found.

Stirling Castle viewed from Bannockburn – urban development is likely to have encroached on the battle area

A number of factors conspire against discovering the site, including the scale of the area over which the armies fought and the thoroughness of the looting. Near contemporary sources are few and frustratingly vague on topography – a wood, a kirk, the Bannock Burn, a park, the Carse, a dry field, a great ditch, and the River Forth. Farmers and builders have churned up the soil over the centuries without any notion of what may lie underneath.

Most people agree that the first day of fighting was around New Park, roughly where the Trust's visitor centre is located today. Aerial photographs reveal the line of the Roman road as far as the southern edge of Bannockburn, where it is buried under urban development. Where the second day's fighting took place is much more contentious, with up to eight potential sites identified from written sources. One theory is that the battlefield was on the Carse between the Pelstream Burn and the Bannock Burn. Another possibility is the Dryfield, an area of drier ground to the south-west of the Carse, now largely covered by housing and Bannockburn High School.

Where was the 'great ditch' referred to by one chronicler as witness to so many deaths among Edward's troops? Some people argue that the reference is to the gorge through which the Bannock Burn emerges onto the Carse; others take the view that it could be any part of the Pelstream Burn or the Bannock Burn as they meander across the Carse towards the river.

All that is certain is that this is the place that has been set aside and preserved for the nation by the Trust to remember Bannockburn.

Tony Pollard and Neil Oliver with volunteers digging on the Carse

The archaeological quest for Bannockburn

Tony Pollard

Not surprisingly, many people assume that the site of the Battle of Bannockburn is marked by Pilkington Jackson's striking statue of Robert the Bruce on his horse. The statue in fact marks the location of part of the Scottish army's position prior to the battle, one that would have allowed Bruce to control the Roman Road along which Edward II's army approached Stirling.

A major subject of debate among historians has been the location of the main battle, which took place on 24 June 1314 – the day after initial encounters, including the combat between Bruce and de Bohun. Several possible locations have been suggested for the main engagement, but only two of these merit serious consideration. The first is on the Carse, the broad expanse of flat ground which fringes the River Forth and accommodates the meandering course of the Bannock Burn (a stream). The second is on the high ground overlooking the Carse, sandwiched between the high point occupied by the statue and the ridgeline, which drops steeply down to the Carse to the east (this area is sometimes referred to as the Dryfield).

One tool that can perhaps settle this debate is battlefield archaeology, which has provided evidence for the location of a number of British battles, including the Battle of Bosworth (1485), where finds of cannonballs proved the true location to be around one and a half miles away from where it had long been claimed. However, with a battle as old as Bannockburn the chances of finding objects relating to the fight, such as arrowheads and pieces of armour, are greatly reduced. For one thing, iron will rust to almost nothing over time, especially in the wet and dry conditions which prevail on the Carse, and for another, many items will have been collected up in the days and years after the battle to be used again or recycled.

Despite these challenging circumstances, an archaeological project, carried out by the Centre for Battlefield Archaeology in partnership with GUARD Archaeology Ltd and sponsored by the National Trust for Scotland and the BBC, took place in 2012 and 2013 with the aim of settling the debate once and for all. This ambitious exercise saw metal detector surveys carried out across both the Carse and the high ground overlooking it. At the time of writing the survey is still underway and as yet no obviously tell-tale finds have been made in either area.

Metal detecting was always going to be a long shot with a 700-year-old battle, but battlefield archaeology has other weapons in its armoury and these have helped to shed important new light on our understanding of where the battle took place.

A number of locations on the Carse were test pitted. This involved digging small trenches through the topsoil down onto the subsoil beneath it, thus allowing for the recovery of any objects in the soil, and this time not just those made from metal. There was also a chance that this would expose any archaeological features, such as pits or hearths. An obvious target for any archaeological project on a battlefield are the graves in which the dead were buried but again these are notoriously difficult to locate, not least because a lot of bodies will fit in a small pit. The small trial pits did not expose any graves but did result in the recovery of sherds of medieval pottery.

Volunteers hard at work digging test pits on the Carse

Silver Edward I penny found during metal detector survey at Cambuskenneth Abbey, where Robert Bruce kept his baggage train during the battle

These date to roughly the time of the battle and provide the first archaeological evidence of human settlement on the Carse during the 14th century. One of the arguments against the battle being fought on the Carse is that it was little more than a peat bog in 1314. We now know that even though parts of the Carse would have been boggy it was occupied by settlements, with farming taking place, and thus may have appeared, to the English especially, as suitable ground on which to give battle.

The landscape is a key to understanding where and how a battle was fought, and another technique utilised by archaeologists is LiDAR, which uses lasers to accurately record the nature of the ground, producing a 3D computer model of the landscape. Recent features can then be removed in order to get a better idea of how the place appeared at the time of the battle. This is especially important at Bannockburn, where modern development in the form of housing estates, schools, roads and railways have cluttered the landscape, making it very difficult to see how one terrain feature relates to another.

Using this technique, it is possible to identify the most likely routes taken by Edward's army down onto the Carse where he camped the night before the battle (this is mentioned in the medieval accounts of the battle). This analysis also suggests that his army was unlikely to have moved back onto the high ground to do battle the following morning. The slope up which the English army would have had to climb, to meet the Scots on the high ground, is steep, and was probably wooded (as suggested by environmental studies). So it would seem almost foolhardy to attempt to negotiate it with horses and thousands of men, and risk being attacked by the Scots while doing so.

Corroded iron object found at Bannockburn in 2004, which may be an artefact from the time of the battle

At present the evidence might not definitively point to one site in favour of the other, but we are confident that the net is closing. For the English under Edward II Bannockburn was a battle lost, but hopefully for us it will ultimately be a battle found.

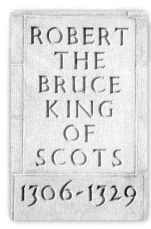

Pilkington Jackson working on his iconic statue of Robert Bruce in the studio in 1964 (J Valentine & Co)

Flying the flag

From Hastings to Gettysburg, people have commemorated battlefield sites which marked a turning point in their history. Bannockburn has become a symbol of Scotland's enduring struggle to define itself, and remains synonymous in the Scottish psyche with identity and nationhood. Lodged deep within the collective memory and expressed in poems, songs and paintings, Bannockburn is part of Scotland's cultural inheritance. In the absence of a Scottish national anthem, it is often the Corries' 1968 folksong, *Flower of Scotland*, celebrating the victory, that the crowds sing at international sporting events.

There was only one eyewitness who wrote about the battle. After being captured, Robert Baston, a poet Edward had chosen to accompany his army, was made to write a poem praising the victors. Over the ensuing centuries 'spin doctors' on both sides, most of whom were clerics with little understanding of military tactics, took up the story. Their 'histories' placed more emphasis on chivalry than carnage. In his biographical epic *The Brus*, 14th-century poet John Barbour wrote a colourful and detailed account of events, although he was a child when they occurred and his version should not be accepted without question.

We can only imagine the people who may have visited the Borestone over the centuries. The earliest known account comes from letters written by traveller John Macky, describing his experience in 1723: '*On my road, near a village called St Ringin* [St Ninians], *remains the stone, in which King Robert Bruce's standard was fixed, at the famous battel of Bannockburn*'. Robert Burns paid his respects at the Borestone during his tour of Scotland in 1787. He noted down old Scottish tunes including *Tutti Tatti*, the battle march of Bruce's men at Bannockburn which later became *Scots Wha Hae*. With his powerful combination of romance and storytelling, Walter Scott finished his poem *The Lord of the Isles* with an account of the battle. Artists began to sketch the Borestone and picture the battle.

From the creative impulse to reshape Scotland's past came the desire to mark its key events with memorials, and a flagstaff was erected at the Borestone in the 19th century. Bannockburn was soon firmly on the tourist route, thanks in part to cheap rail travel, and visitors wrote postcards home describing their Bannockburn experience. By 1929 the site was so popular that Stirling Council considered opening a museum and tearoom there.

However, by then part of the site around the Borestone was at risk of being built over. The Earl of Elgin and Kincardine, head of the Bruce family, set up a national committee to raise funds to buy 23 hectares (58 acres) of the site. Fundraising stalled due to the Depression and the onset of the Second World War. In 1943 the National Trust for Scotland was gifted the Borestone for the nation.

After a worldwide Bannockburn appeal, the Trust gave the site a more monumental quality, having previously rejected suggestions for a diorama, tower and battle hall. It commissioned the creation of the Rotunda as a backdrop to the monuments and to focus attention on Stirling Castle, Edward's goal on that momentous midsummer's day.

Her Majesty, Queen Elizabeth II marked the 650th anniversary of the battle by unveiling the giant bronze equestrian statue of Robert the Bruce by Pilkington Jackson. The sculptor's powerful portrayal has since become a Scottish icon, recognised worldwide.

'By oppression's woes and pains,
By your sons in servile chains,
We will drain our dearest veins,
But they shall be free!
Lay the proud usurpers low!
Tyrants fall in every foe!
Liberty's in every blow!
Let us do, or die!'

Robert Burns, *Scots Wha Hae*, 1794

Commemorating the site

Andrew Wright

In the compelling story of re-establishing Scotland's national identity, the commemoration of the site known as the Borestone, where in June 1314 King Robert I is widely believed to have planted his battle standard, deserves more than a passing mention. For many, and for so long, the round millstone resting on the verge of a country lane was the only tangible reminder of a battle that changed the course of history. First recorded in 1723, it became a place of pilgrimage and was to fire the imagination of generations of poets and artists. Robert Burns was inspired to compose the verses of *Scots Wha Hae* after a visit here in 1787, and among the first illustrations we have of the stone is a fine etching by Andrew Geddes in 1826. In his footsteps followed J M W Turner on his tour of Scotland in 1834, preparing pencil sketches of the Borestone with the framed view of Stirling Castle.

The stone suffered the lot of many battlefield relics, and it is an unexpected source to which we turn for an account of its popular fate – Bradshaw's *Descriptive Railway Handbook* of 1863:

'... so highly is this stone valued by the Scottish people, that fragments of it are frequently cut off, and set in rings, brooches, &c., and worn as a memorial of one of the proudest days in the annals of Scotland.'

Such was the damage caused to the stone that the landowner erected an iron grille in 1836 to protect it from further harm. The cage remained in position until the site was reconfigured in 1964 by architect Robert Matthew with his ambitious scheme for the Rotunda and the crowning moment of Pilkington Jackson's equestrian statue.

Early 20th-century colour picture postcard showing the flagstaff and Borestone, with the guide's hut in the background

Stirling Castle and St Ninians from the Battlefield of Bannockburn,
sketch by J M W Turner (1834)

By the middle of the 19th century, a pressing desire to commemorate the battle had seen a flagstaff erected at the roadside, to be seen at a distance for those paying homage. In a flush of rising nationalistic pride this was replaced in 1870 by the imposing 120ft tall wrought iron flagpole, forged by the skilled hands of workers from the Clydeside shipyards, the joint gift of the lodges of the Oddfellows of Dumbarton and Stirling. Currently we have no real idea as to how the mast was transported from the Clyde, nor even how it was erected with such precision within such a short space of time. The accompanying celebrations of this event were not welcomed in all quarters, however, and the commemoration of a famous victory over the English was seen by some newspaper editors in the south as a 'fresh insult'. Such an interpretation seemed to be far from the intentions of those who donated their handiwork.

Over time the site was manicured. Mown grass to the road verges and clipped hedging appeared, with park benches placed for visitors. A corrugated iron hut was erected for the Borestone guide who appeared in popular picture postcards, greeting visitors in his peaked cap. In the 1930s, although the Trust had an interest in Bannockburn from the outset which coincided with the acquisition of the monuments at Glenfinnan and Culloden, funding an appropriate commemorative scheme had to wait until Britain's austerity years had passed in the mid-1950s. The impetus came not from within the Trust, but from the vision of the sculptor Charles d'Orville Pilkington Jackson. He wished to create an equestrian statue to honour Robert Bruce, with the events of the battle recorded in a state-of-the-art diorama for the visitors to the site. The Trust baulked at the ambition of the scheme. In desperation at the inertia, the Merchant Guild of Stirling erected the memorial cairn in 1957, upon which is inscribed the stirring words from the Declaration of Arbroath. The Trust finally seized the initiative, and the present scheme was inaugurated in time for the 650th anniversary of the battle in 1964, of which the origins are to be found in the sculptor's inspiration for the celebration of the hilltop site.

And the Borestone? It is an irony that the only tangible relic of the battle to which visitors flocked in large numbers remained vulnerable. The last fragments had to be rescued in 1967 from its shattered glass case. They have been given pride of place in the displays of the new visitor centre, and the exact location of the Borestone on the hilltop site is marked with a commemorative stone.

Front page of the 'Guide to the Great Scottish National Panorama – Battle of Bannockburn', published in 1800

Telling the story

Interpretation helps us to imagine the cut and thrust of the battle and to visualise the battlefield within the very different landscape of today.

Possibly the earliest attempt to visualise the battle was the diorama produced by the Scottish National Panorama Company in the early 1800s. For the investment of three pence, pleasure seekers in Scottish cities could visit the Great Scottish Panorama: Battle of Bannockburn, which was open daily from 9am to 11pm. According to its promoters, the work was intended 'to arouse or revive in the breast of every beholder the memories of Scotland's Heroes and of the most glorious and momentous event in Scottish History'.

The Trust opened an auditorium and information centre at Bannockburn on the 650th anniversary of the battle and five years later visitors could enjoy an audio-visual presentation. With more and more people discovering Bannockburn, 1982 saw a new tape-slide show and an extension to the centre in partnership with the Scottish Tourist Board. Five years later the Trust mounted a permanent exhibition, including replica weapons which visitors could try out for themselves, tableaux of key events and a model of the battlefield. New layers of experience were introduced, with Living History actors bringing the story to life for school children and a film drawing on battlefield re-enactments.

With the 700th anniversary of Bannockburn on the horizon, the Trust decided that it was time to apply 21st-century technology to add both drama and reality to one of the greatest stories of Scottish history. A £9m

award from the Heritage Lottery Fund and the Scottish Government to the Trust in partnership with Historic Scotland financed the replacement of the former Bannockburn Heritage Centre, the restoration of the Rotunda and landscaping to create a stronger and more emotive link between the two focal points. A specially commissioned poem composed by Kathleen Jamie has been inscribed on the new ring beam of the Rotunda, fulfilling the original intentions of the designer half a century ago.

From near-contemporary accounts to the film *Braveheart*, the Bannockburn story has been coloured by propaganda, romance and the love of a good story. The Trust, therefore, recruited some of the UK's top experts on the Battle of Bannockburn to inform and guide the interpretation. Their collective knowledge lies behind the re-creation of battle scenes by the Centre for Digital Documentation and Visualisation (a partnership between The Glasgow School of Art's Digital Design Studio and Historic Scotland). Core to the experience is motion capture technology, famously used in the *Lord of the Rings* trilogy. Re-enactors use prop weapons made of plastic to engage in a real fight, provoking genuine reactions and emotions, that are all digitally captured and then used to realistically animate the 3D battle characters. More complex battle sequences are created by combining the motion capture data with special effects at a later stage in production.

Visitors can be in the thick of medieval battle in a way that has never been achieved before – vicious, noisy and real.

Above and below: the Battle Room in the new visitor centre

ALLOA TOWER
Alloa Park, Alloa, Clackmannanshire FK10 1PP

Dating from the 14th century, Alloa Tower is Scotland's largest and oldest keep and the ancestral home of the influential Erskine family, the Earls of Mar and Kellie. The Tower has been altered over the centuries, and is now an 18th-century mansion within a medieval shell. Unusual features include a sweeping Italianate staircase, a double groin-vaulted ceiling and a medieval dungeon. There is also an important collection of portraits, silver and furniture, which are loaned from the family's private collections.

DIRECTIONS: Off A907, 6 miles (9.5km) east of Stirling
OPEN: Easter to 31 October (see website for opening times)
TEL: 01259 211701
DISTANCE: 10 miles (16km) from the Battle of Bannockburn Visitor Centre

ROYAL BURGH OF CULROSS
Culross, Fife KY12 8JH

This historic 17th-century port on the River Forth was once a hive of industry thanks to coal mining, salt panning and the now obsolete trade of iron girdle making. Explore the beautifully refurbished palace, which dates from 1597, with original painted woodwork and 17th- and 18th-century furniture. The reconstructed early 17th-century palace garden is full of period herbs, fruit and vegetables, all of which have been grown in Scotland for centuries.

DIRECTIONS: Off A985, 6 miles (9.5km) west of Dunfermline
OPEN: Easter to 31 October (see website for opening times)
TEL: 01383 880359
DISTANCE: 15 miles (24km) from the Battle of Bannockburn Visitor Centre

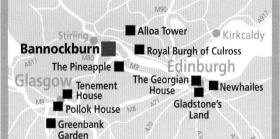

The National Trust for Scotland would like to thank the following for their generous support of The Battle of Bannockburn

The Scottish Government
Riaghaltas na h-Alba

heritage lottery fund
LOTTERY FUNDED